# KIDS CAN COOK
## VEGETARIAN

Button Books

Illustrated by Esther Coombs

# CONTENTS

3 Before you begin
4 Equipment
5 Basic techniques

## Snacks & sides
8 Dips
10 Vegetable crisps
11 Muffin pizzas
12 Potato tots
14 Sweet potato rösti
16 Baked courgette fries

## Main meals
18 Breakfast burritos
20 Tomato soup
21 Falafel
22 Roasted vegetable bowls
24 Frittata
26 Ratatouille
27 Halloumi burgers
28 Bean burgers
30 Carrot hot dogs
32 Veggie nuggets
34 Spinach lasagne
36 Mac & cheese
38 Spaghetti & veggie balls
40 Cauliflower crust pizza
42 Courgetti
44 Rainbow skewers
46 Veggie sausages & mash
48 Thai green curry
50 Katsu curry
52 Mixed bean chilli

## Sweet treats
54 Blueberry pancakes
55 Banana pancakes
56 Courgette brownies
58 Butternut squash cookies
60 Chocolate & beetroot cake
62 Fruit & root roll-ups

## Key
Look out for these symbols in the book. They tell you if a recipe is vegan or gluten-free.

 Vegan (meat, fish, dairy and egg-free)

 Gluten-free

# BEFORE YOU BEGIN

Get ready to have lots of fun in the kitchen, learning basic cooking skills and making delicious vegetarian things for you, your family and your friends to eat.

Before you start, read through the recipe first to make sure you've got all the ingredients and equipment you need, and you understand what you'll be doing. If you need to prepare any ingredients (such as peeling or slicing), do this before you start to cook. And never start cooking without the help of an adult!

## Using an oven/microwave oven

If you need to move any of the oven shelves, do this before turning it on. Cook food on the middle shelf of the oven, unless the recipe says otherwise.

Don't open the oven door until the cooking time is up, unless you think something might be burning. Always wear oven gloves when taking anything out of a microwave or oven.

## STAYING SAFE

* Make sure there's an adult there to help you.

* Always wash your hands before you start cooking, and when you've finished.

* If you're wearing rings, take them off.

* Tie long hair back and wear an apron.

* Be very careful when using a sharp knife or vegetable peeler.

* Never leave the kitchen when the hob is on.

* Use oven gloves when handling anything hot, and put hot dishes onto a trivet or heatproof mat.

* Turn pot handles to the side of the hob to keep them safely out of the way

* Be very careful when boiling things.

Before you begin **3**

# EQUIPMENT

You don't need loads of fancy equipment to make the recipes in this book, but here are some really useful things to have in your kitchen.

Fish slice
Measuring jug
Food processor
Kitchen scales
Whisk
Oven gloves
Box grater
Large mixing bowl
Wooden spoon
Vegetable peeler
Garlic press
Baking tray
Large metal spoon
Potato masher
Sharp knife
Cake tin
Chopping board
Citrus squeezer

Kids Can Cook Vegetarian

# BASIC TECHNIQUES

### How to chop an onion
Put the onion on a chopping board and cut off the top. Use a sharp knife to cut in half through the root. Remove the papery outer skin.

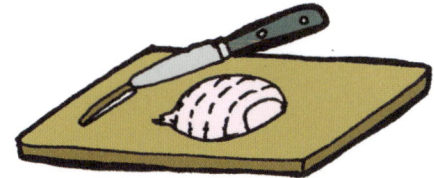

Place one half of the onion flat side down and hold it firmly, with the root pointing towards your little finger. Cut across the onion to make slices and discard the end with the root.

To make the onion slices into dice, cut the other way across the onion.

### How to chop an avocado
Put the avocado on a chopping board. Using a sharp knife, cut in half from top to bottom.

Lift the stone out with a dessertspoon and discard.

Run the spoon around the edge of the flesh and remove from the skin.

Place flat side down and cut into slices. Cut the other way to make the slices into dice.

### How to deseed a pepper
Cut the top off the pepper. You will see the core and seeds inside. Use a sharp knife to cut away the parts of the core attached to the pepper and pull away.

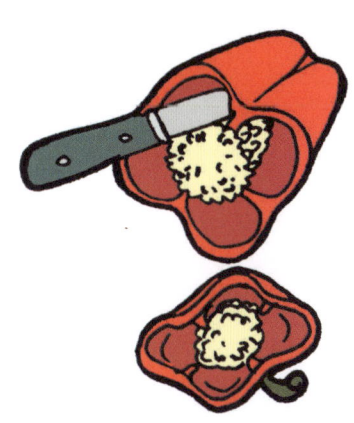

Basic techniques 5

### How to chop a butternut squash

Put the squash on a chopping board and use a sharp knife to cut off the top and bottom.

Run a vegetable peeler from top to bottom to remove the skin.

Stand the squash upright on the board and cut in half.

Use a dessertspoon to scoop out the seeds and any stringy bits.

Lay one half flat side down on the board and cut into slices. To make the slices into dice, cut the other way across the squash.

### How to crush garlic

Cut the ends off a clove of garlic and peel it. Put it inside a garlic press and squeeze the handles together tightly. Use the back of a knife (not the blade) to scrape off any crushed garlic that is still sticking to it.

### How to use a box grater

Place the grater on a chopping board and hold it firmly by the handle. Hold the vegetable (or cheese) in the other hand and rub up and down the grater. Be very careful that you don't catch your fingers or knuckles on the grater!

Kids Can Cook Vegetarian

### How to crack an egg
Hold the egg in one hand, over a cup or bowl. Tap the middle of the egg with a knife to crack it.

Push your thumbs into the crack and pull apart. Let the insides fall into the cup.

It's best to crack eggs into a separate cup before adding to your mixture in case bits of shell fall in there too!

### How to beat an egg
Put your bowl on top of a damp cloth to stop it moving around. Beat the egg with a fork or whisk until it's frothy.

### How to sift flour
You need to sift flour to get rid of any large lumps. Put a sieve over a large bowl and spoon in the flour. Lift the sieve slightly and shake it from side to side. You may need to use a spoon to rub any large bits of flour through the sieve.

### How to fold in
Use a large metal spoon to gently mix the ingredients. Move the spoon around the edge of the bowl, then fold the mixture over the centre and cut down through the middle. Repeat until everything is well mixed.

Basic techniques

# DIPS

Serve these dips with crackers, tortilla chips, breadsticks or toast. Or, cut a selection of your favourite vegetables into sticks - carrot, celery, pepper and cucumber are all great for dipping. Each dip is enough for 4-6 people.

## HUMMUS

### Ingredients
1 x 400g can chickpeas, drained and rinsed
1 small garlic clove, peeled
1 tbsp tahini
juice of 1 lemon
1 tbsp extra virgin olive oil
pinch of salt

**1** Tip the drained and rinsed chickpeas into a food processor.

**2** Add the garlic clove, tahini, half the lemon juice, oil and salt. Blend until smooth.

**3** If the hummus looks too thick, add a little more lemon juice and blend again.

**4** Using a spatula, scrape into a bowl. Serve straight away, or cover and store in the refrigerator for up to 4 days.

Kids Can Cook Vegetarian

# GUACAMOLE

## Ingredients

2 ripe large avocados, halved and stoned
juice of 1 lime
pinch of salt
½ red chilli, seeds removed and finely chopped
5 cherry tomatoes, quartered (optional)
handful of coriander leaves, roughly chopped (optional)

**1** Using a dessertspoon, scoop out the avocado flesh and put into a bowl. Mash with a fork until smooth.

**2** Stir in the lime juice and salt.

**3** Add the chilli, tomatoes and coriander, if using. Gently stir to combine. Serve, or cover and store in the refrigerator for up to 2 days.

# TOMATO SALSA

## Ingredients

4 ripe medium tomatoes, chopped
¼ red onion, finely chopped
½ red chilli, finely chopped
2 tbsp extra virgin olive oil
1 tbsp red wine vinegar
squeeze of lime juice
handful of mint leaves, finely chopped
handful of chives, finely chopped
pinch of salt

**1** Put all the ingredients in a bowl and mix well. Serve straight away, or cover and store in the refrigerator for up to 5 days.

Snacks & sides

# VEGETABLE CRISPS

## Ingredients
1 parsnip
1 sweet potato
1 large beetroot
3 tbsp sunflower oil
salt and pepper

SERVES 4

**1** Heat the oven to 200°C/ fan 180°C/gas mark 6. Using a vegetable peeler (or the slicer on a box grater), make long, thin slices of parsnip, sweet potato and beetroot.

**2** Pat the slices dry with kitchen paper, then place each vegetable into a separate bowl.

**3** Drizzle 1 tbsp oil into each bowl and season with salt and pepper. Mix until well coated.

**4** Put the slices on 3 separate baking trays, making sure they don't overlap. Bake for 20–25 minutes until crisp.

**5** Transfer to a wire rack to cool. Store in an airtight container.

## Tips
* Beetroot juice stains, so it's a good idea to put on a pair of rubber or plastic gloves before you start.

* Some vegetables cook faster than others, so check each tray individually to make sure they don't burn.

Kids Can Cook Vegetarian

# MUFFIN PIZZAS

## Ingredients
4 English muffins, split in half (or 8 crumpets)
4 tbsp passata
1 ball of vegetarian mozzarella, grated
handful of basil leaves

MAKES 8

EXTRA TOPPING IDEAS
* sweetcorn * pineapple * olives
* finely sliced mushrooms, peppers, courgettes or onions
* vegetarian Cheddar cheese

**1** Put the muffins in the toaster. Lightly toast on both sides.

**2** Heat the grill. Put the toasted muffins on a baking tray.

**3** Spread ½ tbsp passata onto each muffin. Sprinkle with grated mozzarella and top with a few basil leaves.

**4** Cook for 2–3 minutes until the cheese has melted and is golden brown and bubbling.

Snacks & sides  **11**

 # POTATO TOTS

Potato tots are made from grated potato and are shaped into little cylinders. They are crispy on the outside, soft on the inside and very moreish!

## Ingredients

4 tbsp vegetable oil, plus extra for greasing
2 large floury potatoes, such as Maris Pipers, peeled and quartered
1 tbsp chickpea flour (or other gluten-free flour), plus extra for dusting
salt and pepper

MAKES 20

**1** Bring a large pan of salted water to the boil. Add the potatoes, bring back to the boil and cook for 5 minutes. Drain and allow to cool.

**2** Heat the oven to 200°C/fan 180°C/gas mark 6. Grease 2 baking trays.

**3** Once the potatoes are cool enough to handle, grate them into a bowl, using the large holes on a box grater. Stir in the flour. Season with salt and pepper.

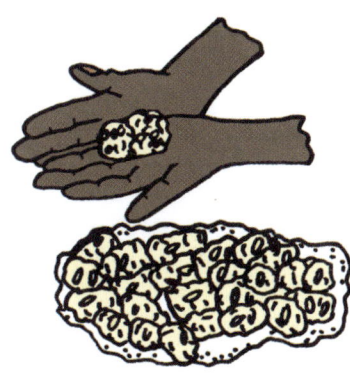

**4** Dust your hands and the work surface with flour. Shape the potato mixture into 20 small cylinders (short sausage shapes). Each potato tot should be about 5cm long.

**5** Heat 2 tbsp of the oil in a large frying pan over a medium heat. Add 10 tots to the pan. Fry for 1–2 minutes on each side until golden brown all over. Remove from the pan. Heat the rest of the oil, then fry the remaining tots in the same way.

**6** Place the tots on the greased baking trays. Bake for 10–15 minutes until soft in the middle and crisp on the outside. Transfer to a plate lined with kitchen paper to soak up any grease.

### Tip

If you're not following a gluten-free diet, you can replace the chickpea flour with 1 tbsp plain flour.

Snacks & sides

# SWEET POTATO RÖSTI

These Swiss potato cakes are delicious topped with sliced avocado and roasted cherry tomatoes. Rösti are traditionally eaten for breakfast, but they are the perfect side to any dish you enjoy eating with potatoes.

## Ingredients

2 large sweet potatoes, peeled
2 tbsp chickpea flour (or other gluten-free flour)
2 tbsp vegetable oil
salt and pepper

SERVES 4

**1** Lay a clean tea towel on the work surface. Grate the potatoes onto the tea towel, using the largest holes on a box grater.

**2** Pick up the corners of the tea towel and twist them together, squeezing the potato into a ball. Hold the tea towel over a bowl and squeeze out as much liquid as possible.

**3** Tip the potato into a large clean bowl. Stir in the flour and season with salt and pepper.

14  Kids Can Cook Vegetarian

  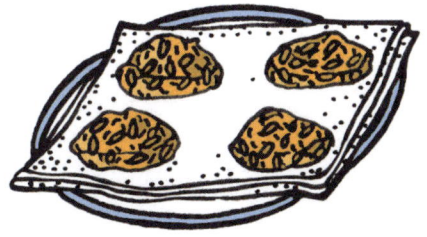

**4** Heat the oil in a large frying pan over a medium heat. Add the potato to the pan in 4 piles, pressing each one down with the back of a spoon.

**5** Fry for 5–10 minutes on each side, turning carefully with a fish slice or spatula, until they are crisp and golden on the outside and soft in the middle.

**6** Transfer the rösti to a plate lined with kitchen paper to soak up any grease.

## Tip

If you're not following a gluten-free diet, you can replace the chickpea flour with 2 tbsp plain flour.

## Variations

Replace 1 sweet potato with 2 grated carrots or 2 grated parsnips, or one of each.

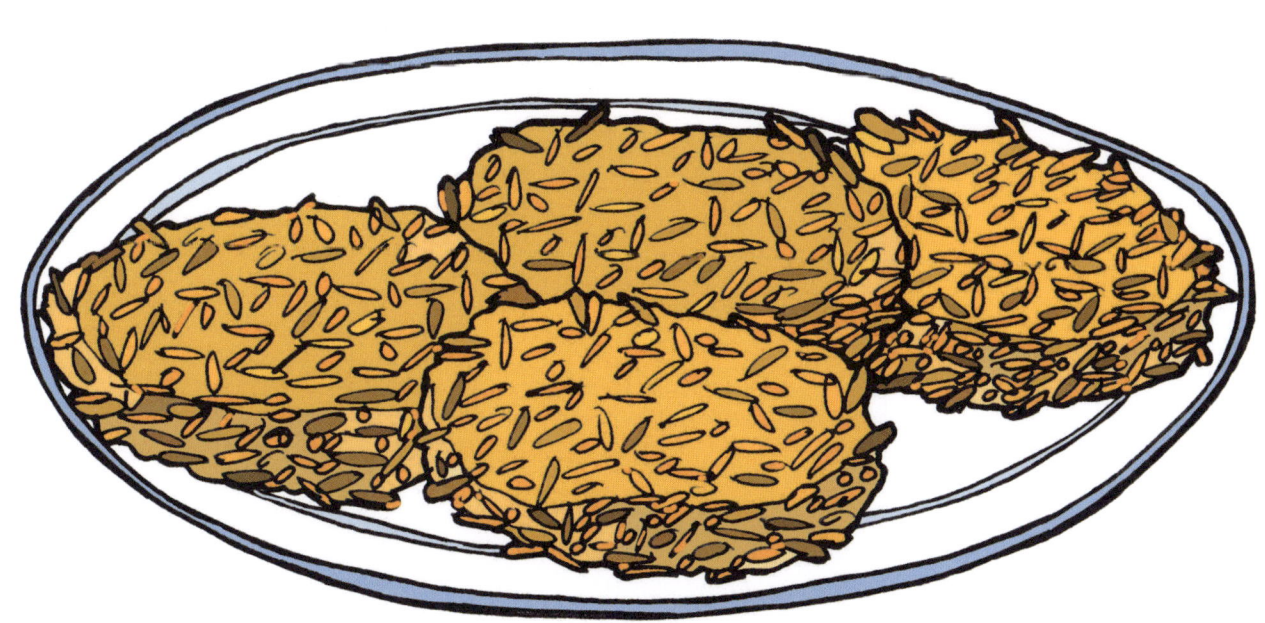

Snacks & sides

# BAKED COURGETTE FRIES

## Ingredients
50g plain flour
2 eggs
50g panko breadcrumbs, crushed
2 medium courgettes, halved widthways and cut into sticks
salt and pepper

SERVES 4

### Tip
To give the fries extra flavour, stir 4 tbsp grated vegetarian Italian-style hard cheese into the breadcrumbs in Step 2.

Kids Can Cook Vegetarian

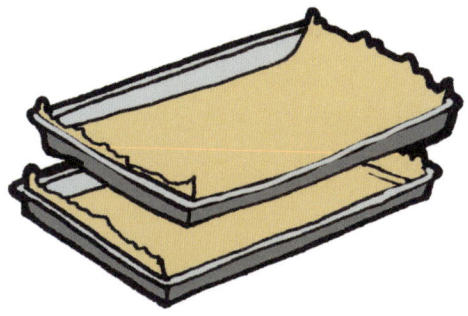

**1** Heat the oven to 220°C/fan 200°C/gas mark 7. Line 2 baking trays with baking paper.

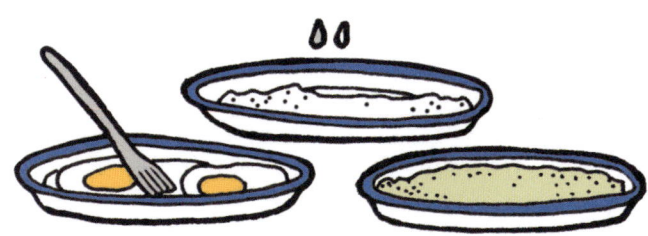

**2** Put 3 wide, shallow bowls on the work surface. Tip the flour into the first bowl and season with salt and pepper. Crack the eggs into the second bowl and beat together with a fork. Tip the breadcrumbs into the third bowl.

**3** Take a courgette stick and coat it in flour, shaking to remove any excess. Dip into the beaten egg, then into the breadcrumbs, making sure it is evenly coated in crumbs.

**4** Lay the breadcrumbed courgette stick on a baking tray. Repeat with the rest of the courgette sticks.

**5** Bake for 10 minutes, then use a pair of tongs to turn the fries over. Return to the oven and bake for 10–15 minutes until the courgette is tender and the coating is crisp and golden.

**6** As soon as the fries are cooked, sprinkle with a little salt and serve.

Snacks & sides

# BREAKFAST BURRITOS

## Ingredients

1 tbsp vegetable oil
1 red pepper, deseeded and sliced
1 x 400g can black beans, drained and rinsed
knob of butter
4 eggs, beaten
4 large flour tortillas, warmed
1 avocado, halved, stoned and sliced, or 1 x quantity Guacamole (see page 9)
100g vegetarian Cheddar cheese, grated
salt and pepper

SERVES 4

## Variation

Try replacing the egg with tofu. Put 400g extra-firm tofu (drained) in a bowl and break into small chunks with a fork. Add to the hot pan in Step 4, cook for 5 minutes, stirring occasionally, then stir in 2 tsp ground turmeric and a little salt. Cook for 3 minutes, stirring frequently, then remove from the heat.

**1** Heat the oil in a large frying pan over a medium heat. Add the pepper and cook, stirring occasionally, for 5 minutes until starting to soften.

**2** Move the pepper to one side of the pan. Tip in the beans. Cook for 2 minutes. Mash the beans lightly with a fork or potato masher, then tip the pepper and mashed beans into a bowl. Cover with a piece of tin foil or a plate and set aside.

**3** Put the same pan back on the heat and add the butter.

**4** Season the beaten eggs with salt and pepper, then pour into the hot pan. Cook for 2–3 minutes, or until just set, stirring occasionally with a wooden spoon and bringing the mixture in from the sides. Once cooked, remove from the heat.

**5** Place a warmed tortilla on a board or plate. Add a spoonful or two of the pepper and bean mixture to the lower half of the tortilla. Top with scrambled egg and a few slices of avocado (or a spoonful of guacamole), then sprinkle with cheese.

**6** Fold in the sides of the tortilla, then fold the bottom up and over the filling. Keep rolling the tortilla up until you get to the top edge. Repeat with the remaining tortillas and filling ingredients. Slice in half and serve.

Main meals

# TOMATO SOUP

## Ingredients

2 tbsp olive oil
1 onion, finely chopped
2 carrots, peeled and finely chopped
2 garlic cloves, crushed
8 fresh tomatoes, chopped
1 x 400g can chopped tomatoes

750ml vegetable stock
handful of basil leaves
salt and pepper

TO SERVE
gluten-free bread or croutons

SERVES 4

**1** Heat the oil in a large pan over a low heat. Fry the onion and carrot for 5–10 minutes until softened. Add the garlic and fry for 2 minutes.

**2** Stir in the fresh tomatoes, tinned tomatoes and stock. Bring to the boil, then turn down the heat. Put a lid on the pan and gently simmer for 20–25 minutes.

**3** Remove from the heat and stir in half of the basil leaves. Using a stick blender, blend the soup until smooth. Season with a little salt and pepper.

**4** Stir in the rest of the basil. Ladle into bowls and serve with sliced bread or croutons.

# FALAFEL

## Ingredients

1 x 400g can chickpeas, drained and rinsed
1 garlic clove, crushed
handful of flat-leaf parsley
1 tsp ground cumin
pinch of mild chilli powder
2 tbsp plain flour, plus extra for dusting
pinch of salt
2 tbsp vegetable oil

MAKES 6-8

**1** Tip the chickpeas, garlic, parsley, cumin, chilli powder, flour and salt into a food processor. Blend until the mixture is almost smooth.

**2** Dust your hands and the work surface with a little flour. Shape the mixture into 6–8 evenly sized balls.

**3** Heat the oil in a large frying pan over a medium heat. Fry until golden brown on each side.

**4** Transfer to a plate lined with kitchen paper.

**5** Serve with pitta bread, salad, hummus (see page 8) and a squeeze of lemon juice.

Main meals **21**

# ROASTED VEGETABLE BOWLS

These bowls are packed with goodness. Give this recipe a try and then experiment with any vegetables, grains, salad leaves, dressings and toppings you like.

## Ingredients
3 tbsp olive oil
1 tsp cumin
1 tsp oregano
1 tsp garlic powder
½ butternut squash, peeled, deseeded and chopped into 2cm cubes
1 red onion, peeled and cut into 8 wedges
600ml water
200g quinoa, rinsed
large handful of baby spinach, washed
vegan feta cheese, crumbled (optional)

FOR THE DRESSING
1 tbsp tahini
3 tbsp dairy-free yoghurt
½ tbsp maple syrup

TO SERVE
sesame, pumpkin or sunflower seeds

SERVES 4

 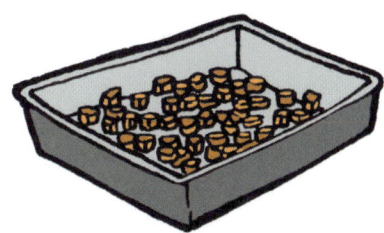 

**1** Heat the oven to 220°C/fan 200°C/gas mark 7. In a large bowl, mix together the oil, cumin, oregano and garlic powder. Add the butternut squash and mix well.

**2** Tip the butternut squash into a large roasting tray. Bake in the oven for 15 minutes.

**3** Remove from the oven, add the onion wedges and bake for 15 minutes, or until tender.

**4** While the vegetables are roasting, cook the quinoa. Pour the water into a large pan and place over a high heat. Bring to the boil, then add the quinoa. Turn the heat to medium. Put the lid on. Cook for 15–20 minutes, or until the water has been absorbed and the quinoa is tender.

**5** To make the dressing, put the tahini in a bowl. Add the yoghurt and syrup. Whisk until smooth.

**6** Divide the ingredients between 4 bowls. Start with a large spoonful of quinoa, then put some squash next to it, then some onion, and finally a handful of spinach. Top with crumbled feta (if using), then drizzle with dressing and sprinkle with seeds.

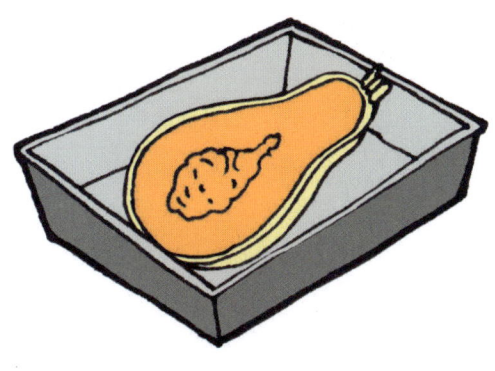

### Tip

You can use the other half of the squash to make delicious cookies! Start by removing the seeds (you can leave the peel on) and placing it on a baking tray. Heat the oven to 220°C/fan 200°C/gas mark 7. Bake for 1 hour, or until tender. Allow to cool completely. Now, turn to page 58 and follow the cookie recipe.

Main meals

# FRITTATA

Frittatas are super easy to make and a great dish to fill with all your favourite vegetables. Very similar to an omelette, they are quick to cook and delicious at any time of the day.

## Ingredients

400g new potatoes, cut into ½cm-thick slices
1 tbsp olive oil
bunch of spring onions, trimmed and finely sliced
1 courgette, sliced
7 large eggs
100g frozen peas, thawed
50g vegetarian Cheddar cheese, grated
salt and pepper

SERVES 4-6

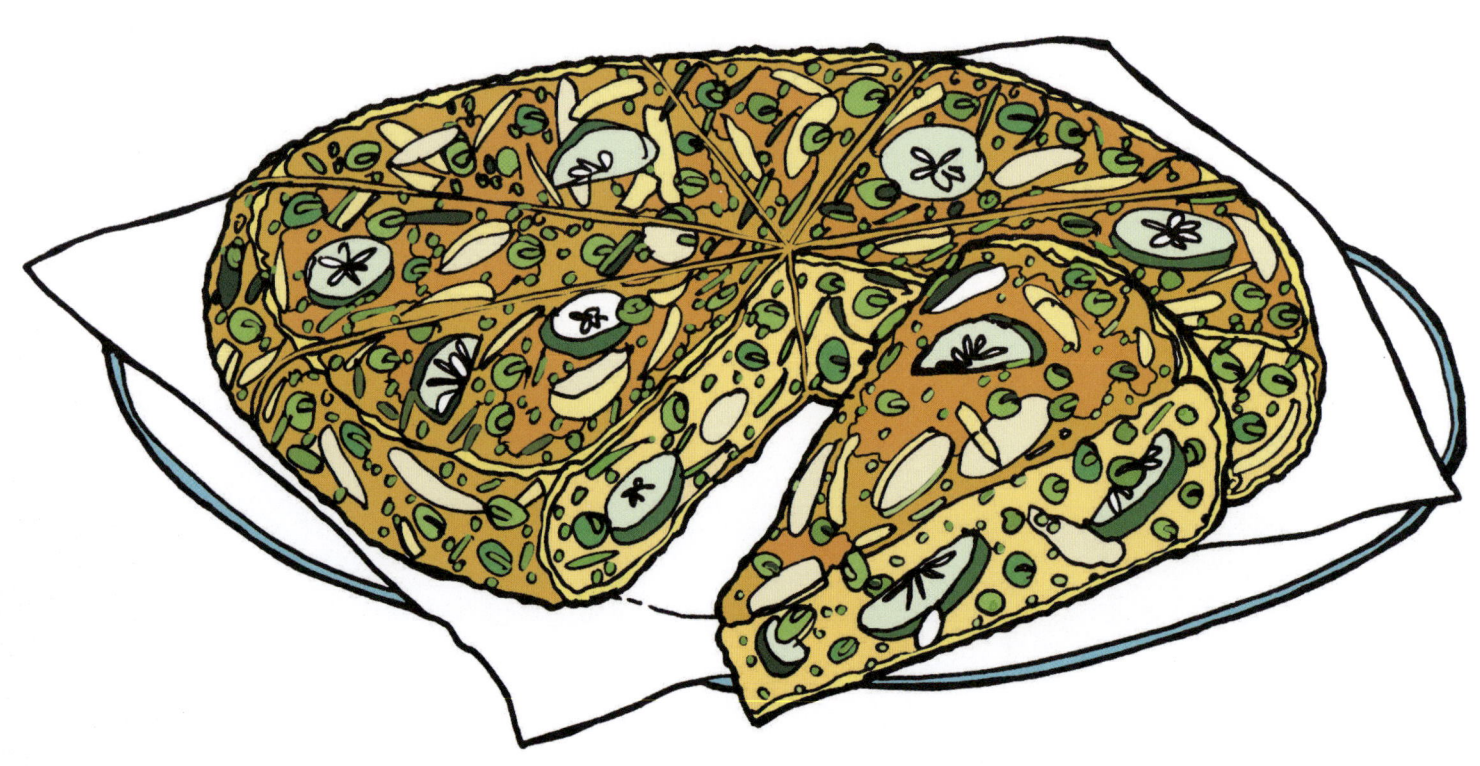

Kids Can Cook Vegetarian

**1** Bring a large saucepan of salted water to the boil. Drop in the potato and cook for 3–4 minutes until just tender. Drain.

**2** Heat the oil in a large ovenproof frying pan over a medium heat. Fry the spring onions for 2–3 minutes until soft.

**3** Add the courgette and potato to the pan. Fry for 3–4 minutes on each side until starting to brown at the edges.

**4** Crack the eggs into a jug. Beat lightly with a fork, then season with salt and pepper.

**5** Pour the beaten egg into the pan. Scatter over the peas and top with the grated cheese. Turn the heat down to low. Cook gently until the egg is almost set (it should still be a little runny on top). Heat the grill.

**6** Place the pan under the preheated grill for 4–5 minutes, or until the egg is set and the cheese has melted.

**7** Cut into slices and serve.

EXTRA TOPPING IDEAS
* pesto (see page 43) * vegetarian goat's cheese
* vegetarian feta cheese * olives * chopped dill,
mint, parsley or basil

Main meals

# RATATOUILLE

Serve this summer vegetable stew with fresh bread or pasta, or spooned over a baked potato.

## Ingredients

2 tbsp olive oil
1 large onion, finely chopped
2 garlic cloves, crushed
2 courgettes, halved lengthways and thickly sliced
2 red peppers, deseeded and diced
1 aubergine, cut into 2½cm chunks

2 x 400g cans chopped tomatoes
1 tbsp mixed dried herbs
salt and pepper

TO SERVE
handful of basil leaves, torn

SERVES 4-6

**1** Heat the oil in a large pan over a low heat. Add the onion and garlic and cook for 5–10 minutes, or until soft.

**2** Stir in the courgette, pepper and aubergine. Cook for 5 minutes, stirring occasionally.

**3** Add the tomatoes and the dried herbs. Put a lid on the pan and cook for 20–25 minutes, or until the vegetables are tender. Remove the lid and cook for 5 minutes to thicken the sauce.

**4** Season with salt and pepper, sprinkle with basil and serve.

26  Kids Can Cook Vegetarian

# HALLOUMI BURGERS

## Ingredients
1 tbsp olive oil
1 x 250g block of vegetarian halloumi cheese, cut into 8 thick slices

TO SERVE
4 burger buns, spilt in half
1 baby gem lettuce, leaves separated
2 tomatoes, sliced
1 x quantity Hummus (see page 8)

SERVES 4

**1** Heat the oil in a large frying pan over a medium heat. Add the halloumi and fry for 2–3 minutes on each side, or until crisp and golden.

**2** Transfer the halloumi to a plate lined with kitchen paper to soak up any grease.

**3** To assemble the burgers, spread some hummus on the bottom half of the bun. Add 2 slices of halloumi, a couple of tomato slices and a few lettuce leaves. Sandwich with the top half of the bun and serve.

## Tip
Toast the burger buns under the grill before filling, if you like.

Main meals 27

# BEAN BURGERS

## Ingredients
1 x 400g can mixed beans, drained and rinsed
2 tbsp vegetable oil
pinch of mild chilli powder, ground cumin or paprika
1 large carrot, grated
1 red onion, finely chopped
2 garlic cloves, crushed
small handful of coriander leaves, roughly chopped
2 tsp plain flour, plus extra for dusting

TO SERVE
6 burger buns, split in half
lettuce
tomato ketchup

SERVES 6

Kids Can Cook Vegetarian

**1** Tip the beans into a saucepan. Cover with cold water. Bring to the boil, then turn down the heat. Simmer for 10 minutes, then drain.

**2** Put the beans into a large bowl. Mash with a potato masher or fork until almost smooth. Set aside.

**3** Heat 1 tbsp of the oil in a large frying pan over a low heat. Stir in your chosen spice. Fry for 1 minute, stirring continuously.

**4** Add the carrot, onion and garlic to the pan. Cook gently for 10 minutes until soft.

**5** Add the carrot and onion mixture to the mashed beans. Put the frying pan to one side (you'll use it again later). Stir in the flour and coriander with a wooden spoon. Leave to cool.

**6** Once the mixture is cool enough to handle, dust your hands and the work surface with flour. Shape the mixture into 6 evenly sized balls.

**7** Wipe the inside of the frying pan with a piece of kitchen paper. Add 1 tbsp of oil and place over a medium heat.

**8** Add the balls to the pan (you might need to cook them in two batches). Flatten with a spatula or fish slice to make them burger shaped. Fry for 5–7 minutes on each side until golden brown.

**9** Put each burger in a bun. Top with lettuce and tomato ketchup.

Main meals

# CARROT HOT DOGS

## Ingredients
1 tbsp maple syrup
½ tbsp olive oil
1 tsp cider vinegar
1 tsp smoked paprika
pinch of salt
4 small carrots, peeled
4 hot dog rolls

SERVES 4

TO SERVE
tomato ketchup
American mustard
crispy kale (see opposite page)

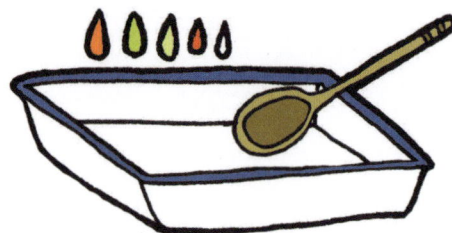

**1** Heat the oven to 200°C/fan 180°C/gas mark 6. Mix together the syrup, oil, vinegar, paprika and salt in a baking dish.

**2** Add the carrots to the dish and toss until evenly coated. Bake in the oven for 30–35 minutes, or until tender.

**3** Open out the hot dog rolls and place on a baking tray. Bake in the oven for 3–5 minutes, or until lightly toasted.

**4** Put a carrot into each toasted roll. Top with ketchup, mustard and a sprinkling of crispy kale.

### Variation
Give these hot dogs a Mexican twist by topping with crushed tortilla chips, salsa, vegan sour cream and grated vegan Cheddar cheese.

Kids Can Cook Vegetarian

## How to make crispy kale

Heat the oven to 150°C/fan 130°C/gas mark 2. Line a baking tray with baking paper. Wash 70g chopped kale. Dry thoroughly with a clean tea towel. Put in a large bowl. Add 1/2 tbsp olive oil and season with salt and pepper. Toss until evenly coated. Tip onto the tray and spread out in a single layer. Bake for 20 minutes, or until crisp but still green.

# VEGGIE NUGGETS

## Ingredients

2 tbsp vegetable oil, plus extra for greasing
1 onion, finely chopped
2 potatoes, peeled
1 garlic clove, crushed
1 carrot, grated
1 parsnip, grated
150g frozen peas, thawed
1 x 200g can sweetcorn, drained
50g plain flour, plus extra for dusting
salt and pepper

SERVES 4

FOR THE COATING
2 eggs, beaten
50g plain flour, plus extra for dusting
100g cornflakes, lightly crushed

## Variation

For a cheesy centre, roll the mixture into balls in Step 6, then take one and flatten it out in the palm of your hand. Put a small cube of vegetarian mozzarella cheese in the centre, then fold over the edges of the mixture to cover. Flatten a little to create a nugget shape, making sure the cheese doesn't poke through. Repeat with the rest of the mixture, then continue from Step 7.

Kids Can Cook Vegetarian

**1** Heat the oil in large frying pan over a low heat. Add the onion and fry for 5–10 minutes, or until softened, stirring occasionally with a wooden spoon.

**2** Using the largest holes on a box grater, grate the potatoes onto a clean tea towel. Pick up the corners and twist together. Hold over a bowl, squeezing out as much liquid as possible.

**3** Add the garlic to the pan and fry for 1 minute, then tip in the potato, carrot and parsnip. Cook for 10 minutes, or until softened, stirring occasionally.

 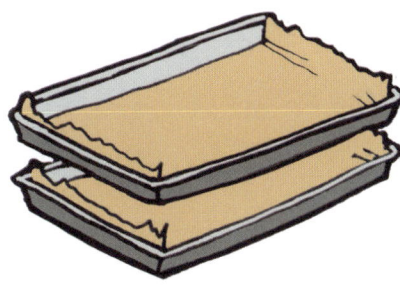 

**4** Tip the vegetables into a large bowl. Stir in the peas, sweetcorn and flour until well mixed. Allow to cool, then cover and put in the refrigerator for 30 minutes.

**5** Heat the oven to 220°C/fan 200°C/gas mark 7. Line 2 baking trays with baking paper.

**6** Remove the mixture from the refrigerator. Season with salt and pepper. Dust your hands and the work surface with flour. Roll into 20 evenly sized balls, then flatten a little to create a nugget shape.

**7** To coat the nuggets, put the eggs, flour and cornflakes into 3 wide, shallow bowls. Season the flour with salt and pepper.

**8** Dip the nuggets into the flour, shaking off any excess, then into the egg, then into the cornflakes. Place on a lined tray.

**9** Bake for 10 minutes. Remove from the oven and turn over with tongs. Bake for 10 minutes, or until crisp and brown.

Main meals

# SPINACH LASAGNE

## Ingredients
800g spinach, washed
200g ricotta, drained
about 300g dried lasagne
   sheets
30g vegetarian Italian-style
   hard cheese, grated
salt and pepper

FOR THE WHITE SAUCE
50g butter
50g plain flour
750ml milk
1 tsp Dijon mustard (optional)

SERVES 6

**1** Put the washed spinach into a sieve or colander. Place over a large bowl. Pour hot water from the kettle over the spinach to wilt (you might need to do this in batches). Leave to cool.

**2** While the spinach is cooling, make the white sauce. Melt the butter in a saucepan over a medium heat. Stir in the flour with a whisk or wooden spoon. Keep stirring for 1 minute, then remove the pan from the heat.

**3** Stir in the milk a little at a time, allowing the sauce to become thick and smooth before adding more milk. Once all the milk has been added, put the pan over a medium heat, stirring continuously. As soon as the sauce comes to the boil, remove from the heat. Stir in the mustard (if using) and season with salt and pepper. Set aside.

**4** Once the spinach is cool enough to handle, take small handfuls and squeeze out as much liquid as possible. Place on a chopping board and finely chop with a sharp knife.

**5** Put the ricotta in a large bowl. Beat with a wooden spoon until smooth. Stir in the chopped spinach and 1 tbsp of the white sauce. Mix well, then season with a little salt and pepper.

**6** Heat the oven to 220°C/fan 200°C/gas mark 7. Spread a little of the spinach mixture over the base of a large, deep baking dish. Cover with a layer of pasta. Spoon over some white sauce and sprinkle with grated cheese. Continue layering in the same way, finishing with a layer of pasta and the rest of the white sauce and grated cheese. Bake in the oven for 30 minutes, or until the top is golden brown and the pasta is soft.

### Tip
If you like your lasagne extra cheesy, sprinkle over 85g grated vegetarian mozzarella or Cheddar cheese before baking.

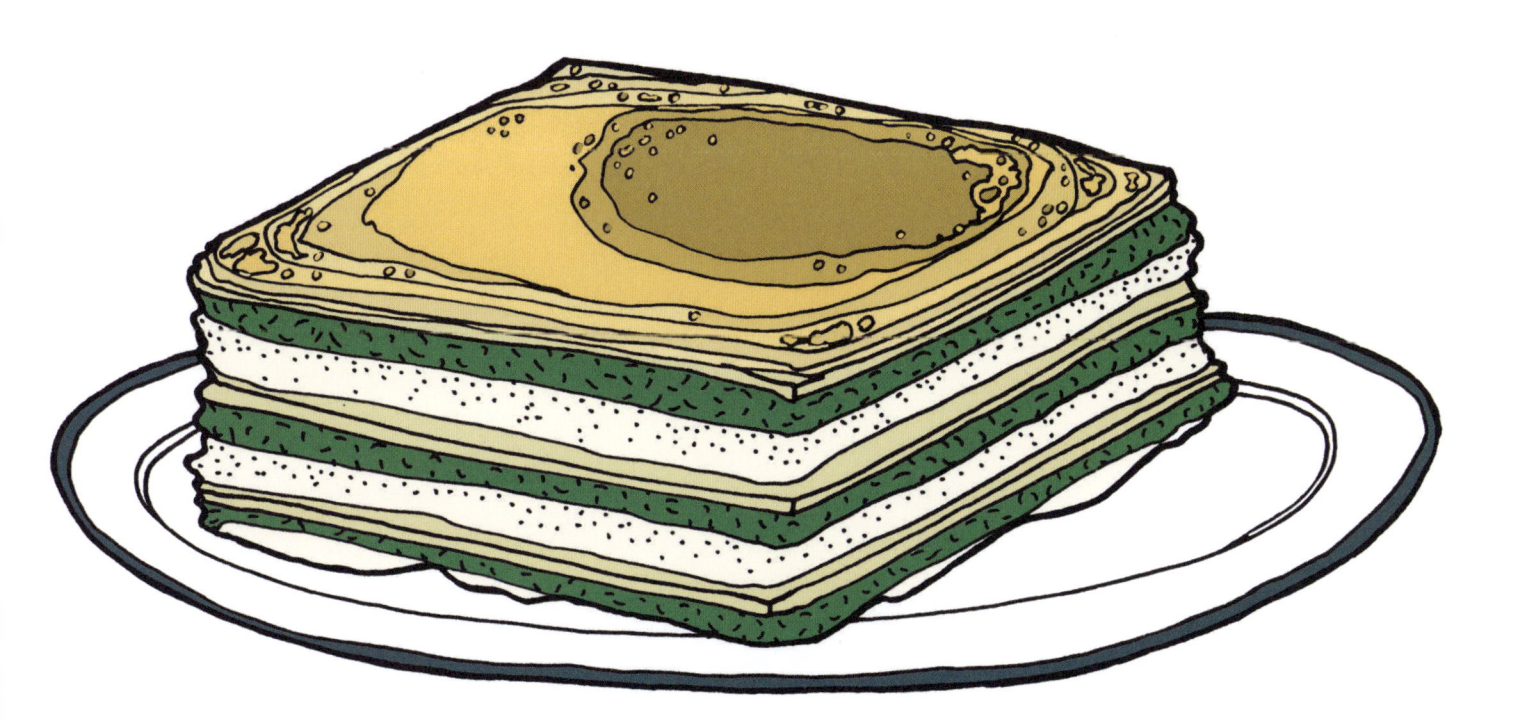

Main meals

# MAC & CHEESE

## Ingredients

200g dried macaroni
40g butter
40g plain flour
500ml milk
50g vegetarian Cheddar cheese, grated, plus extra for sprinkling
1 tsp Dijon mustard (optional)
your chosen vegetable (see below)
salt and pepper

SERVES 4

## VEGETABLE IDEAS

### PEAS
Add 100g frozen peas to the pan 1 minute before the end of the cooking time in Step 1.

### BROCCOLI
Add 200g broccoli (or cauliflower) florets to the pan 5 minutes before the end of the cooking time in Step 1.

### KALE
Add 200g chopped kale to the pan 5 minutes before the end of the cooking time in Step 1.

Kids Can Cook Vegetarian

**1** Heat the oven to 220°C/fan 200°C/gas mark 7. Bring a large saucepan of salted water to the boil. Add the pasta and cook according to the packet instructions, adding your chosen vegetable before the end of the cooking time (see opposite page). Drain, then return to the pan.

**2** To make the cheese sauce, melt the butter in a saucepan over a low heat. Stir in the flour with a wooden spoon or whisk. Cook for 1–2 minutes, stirring all the time. Remove from the heat.

**3** Stir in the milk, a little at a time, allowing the sauce to become thick and smooth before adding more milk. Return to the heat and bring to the boil, stirring continuously. Remove from the heat.

**4** Stir in the cheese, a little salt and pepper, and mustard (if using).

**5** Stir the cheese sauce into the cooked pasta and vegetables and mix well.

**6** Spoon into a large, deep baking dish and sprinkle with cheese. Bake for 8–10 minutes until golden brown and bubbling.

Main meals  **37**

# SPAGHETTI & VEGGIE BALLS

## Ingredients

1 large carrot, peeled and roughly chopped
1 red pepper, deseeded and roughly chopped
1 small red onion, quartered
2 garlic cloves, peeled
1 x 400g can kidney beans, drained and rinsed
100g sweetcorn
50g breadcrumbs
3 tbsp plain flour, plus extra for dusting
2 tbsp olive oil
300g dried spaghetti
salt and pepper

SERVES 4

FOR THE TOMATO SAUCE
1 tbsp olive oil
1 garlic clove, crushed
1 x 400g can chopped tomatoes
handful of basil leaves, plus extra to serve

TO SERVE
nutritional yeast (optional)

**1** Put the carrot, pepper, onion, garlic and kidney beans in a food processor. Blend until everything is very finely chopped.

**2** Tip the vegetables into a large bowl. Stir in the sweetcorn, breadcrumbs and flour with a wooden spoon until well mixed. Season with salt and pepper.

**3** Dust your hands and the work surface with flour. Roll the mixture into 20 evenly sized balls.

Kids Can Cook Vegetarian

**4** Heat the oil in a large pan over a medium heat. Fry the veggie balls for 15–20 minutes, turning occasionally, until cooked through and golden brown all over (you might need to do this in batches). Transfer to a plate lined with kitchen paper to soak up any grease.

**5** To make the tomato sauce, add the oil to the same pan and place over a low heat. Add the garlic and fry for 2 minutes.

**6** Tip in the chopped tomatoes. Half-fill the tin with water and add to the pan. Stir in the basil leaves. Bring to the boil, then turn down the heat so that the sauce is bubbling gently. Cook for 20 minutes, stirring occasionally, until you have a thick sauce.

**7** Turn the heat to low. Season with a little salt and pepper. Drop in the veggie balls so they can heat through while you cook the pasta.

**8** Cook the spaghetti in a large pan of salted water, according to the packet instructions. Drain. Divide between 4 plates. Top with the veggie balls and a few basil leaves, and a sprinkling of nutritional yeast, if you like.

Main meals 39

# CAULIFLOWER CRUST PIZZA

## Ingredients
2 cauliflowers, cut into florets
2 eggs
100g vegetarian Cheddar cheese, finely grated
1 tsp salt
pepper

FOR THE TOPPING
4 tbsp tomato purée
1 ball of mozzarella, sliced
½ red pepper, finely sliced
6 button mushrooms, finely sliced
handful of pitted olives, sliced
1 tsp dried oregano

MAKES 2 MEDIUM PIZZAS

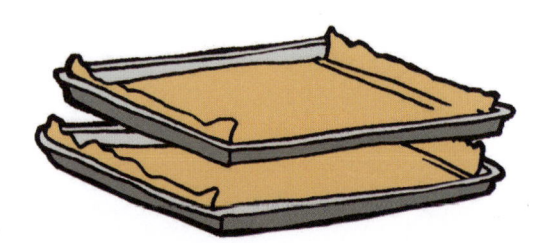

**1** Heat the oven to 180°C/fan 160°C/gas mark 4. Line 2 baking trays with baking paper.

**2** Put the cauliflower in a food processor and blend until very finely chopped (you might need to do this in batches).

**3** Tip the cauliflower into a large dry frying pan. Place over a low heat. Cook for 10–15 minutes, stirring occasionally, until the moisture has evaporated and the cauliflower is dry.

Kids Can Cook Vegetarian

**4** Tip the cauliflower into a large bowl. Add the eggs, cheese, salt and pepper. Stir with a wooden spoon until well mixed.

**5** Divide the mixture evenly between the baking trays. Use the back of a spoon to spread the mixture out evenly and shape into an oval.

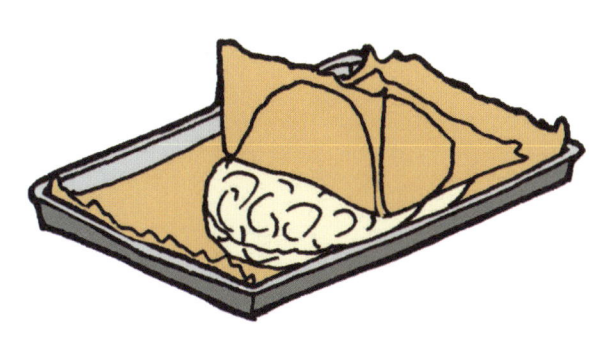

**6** Bake for 30 minutes, or until firm. Wearing oven gloves and holding opposite corners of the baking paper, lift the bases off the trays. Line the trays with fresh paper. Flip the bases over and onto the trays. Peel the paper off the top. Bake for 10 minutes.

**7** Spread on the tomato purée, then top with the cheese, pepper, mushrooms, olives and oregano. Bake for 15 minutes, or until the vegetables are cooked through and the cheese has melted. Slice and serve.

Main meals

# COURGETTI

## Ingredients
4 large courgettes
1 tbsp olive oil
your chosen sauce (see opposite page)

SERVES 4

TO SERVE
vegetarian Italian-style hard cheese, grated (optional)

**1** Make your chosen sauce (see opposite page).

**2** Trim the courgettes, then spiralize them, using the large noodle attachment on your spiralizer (see Tip).

**3** Heat the oil in a large pan over a medium heat.

**4** Add the courgetti and fry for 2–3 minutes to soften.

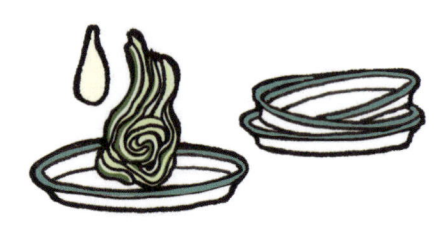

**5** Transfer to 4 plates and spoon over the sauce.

**6** Sprinkle with grated cheese, if you like.

## Tip
If you don't have a spiralizer, use a vegetable peeler to make long, thin strips of courgette. Cut each strip into spaghetti with a sharp knife.

Kids Can Cook Vegetarian

# TOMATO SAUCE

## Ingredients
1 tbsp olive oil
1 garlic clove, crushed
1 x 400g can chopped tomatoes
handful of basil leaves, plus extra to serve
salt and pepper

**1** Heat the oil in a large pan over a low heat. Add the garlic and fry for 1 minute.

**2** Tip in the tomatoes. Half-fill the tin with water and add to the pan. Stir in the basil. Bring to the boil, then turn down the heat and bubble gently. Cook for 20 minutes, stirring occasionally.

**3** Season with salt and pepper and add a little more basil.

# PESTO SAUCE

## Ingredients
40g pine nuts
20g vegetarian Italian-style hard cheese, grated
3 large handfuls of basil
75ml olive oil
1 garlic clove, peeled

**1** Heat a small pan over a low heat. Add the pine nuts and toast gently until just starting to brown. (Keep an eye on them – they burn very quickly!)

**2** Tip the pine nuts, cheese, basil, oil and garlic into a food processor. Blitz until smooth.

Main meals 43

# RAINBOW SKEWERS

## Ingredients
8 cherry tomatoes
1 orange pepper, diced
1 yellow pepper, diced
1 courgette, sliced
1 aubergine, diced

FOR THE GLAZE
2 tbsp olive oil
1 tbsp honey
1 tbsp balsamic vinegar

MAKES 8

### Tip
If you're using wooden skewers, soak them in water for 30 minutes before you start. This will stop them from burning.

**1** To make the glaze, put the oil, honey and vinegar in a bowl and whisk together with a fork.

**2** Thread the vegetables onto the skewers, following the colours of the rainbow. Be careful – skewers have very sharp ends.

**3** Using a pastry brush, brush the vegetables with the glaze. Heat the grill.

**4** Put the skewers under the preheated grill for 10–12 minutes, turning every few minutes.

Kids Can Cook Vegetarian

## Variation

Fruit skewers make a delicious dessert. Try the following:

## Ingredients

16 large white vegan marshmallows
8 small strawberries, stalks and hulls removed
8 mango chunks (fresh or frozen)
8 pineapple chunks (fresh or canned)
2 kiwi fruit, peeled and quartered
16 blueberries

MAKES 8

**1** Thread a marshmallow 'cloud' onto each skewer. Be careful – skewers have very sharp ends.

**2** Thread a strawberry onto each skewer. Add the rest of the fruit, following the colours of the rainbow.

**3** Finish each skewer with a marshmallow. Heat the grill.

**4** Put the skewers under the preheated grill for 10 minutes, turning every few minutes.

## Tip

Drizzle the skewers with your favourite chocolate sauce before serving.

Main meals

# VEGGIE SAUSAGES & MASH

## Ingredients

2 tbsp olive oil, plus extra for brushing
½ onion, finely chopped
2 garlic cloves, crushed
300g chestnut mushrooms, chopped
sprig of thyme, leaves picked
1 x 400g can cannellini beans, drained and rinsed
50g rolled oats
1 tbsp tomato purée
1 tsp smoked paprika
salt and pepper

SERVES 4

FOR THE MASH
4 large floury potatoes, peeled and cut into evenly sized chunks
knob of dairy-free spread
unsweetened coconut milk

**1** Heat 1 tbsp of the oil in a large frying pan over a low heat. Add the onion and fry for 10 minutes until soft. Add the garlic and cook for 1 minute. Tip into a large bowl and set aside.

**2** Add the rest of the oil to the pan. Turn the heat to high. Add the mushrooms and thyme. Cook for 5 minutes, stirring regularly. Tip into the bowl with the onion and garlic. Set aside to cool. (Don't wash up the pan – you'll use it again later.)

**3** To make the mash, place a large pan of cold, salted water over a high heat. Bring to the boil, then add the potatoes. Cook for 15–20 minutes until tender.

Kids Can Cook Vegetarian

**4** Drain in a colander, then set over the pan to steam dry.

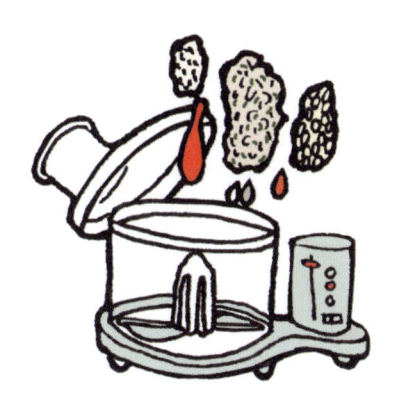

**5** Tip the cooled mushroom mixture into a food processor. Add the beans, oats, tomato purée, paprika, and a little salt and pepper. Blend for a few seconds and then stop. Repeat until well mixed, but the mixture still has some texture (you don't want it to be too smooth).

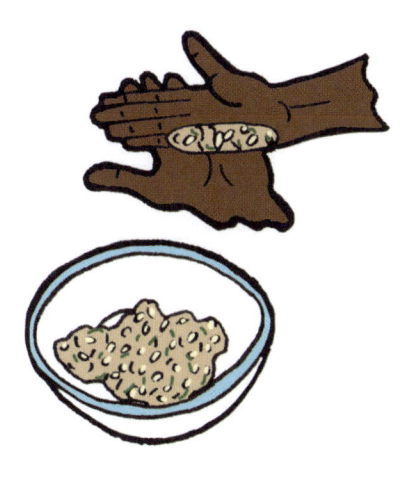

**6** Tip the sausage mixture back into the mixing bowl. Divide the mixture into 8 evenly-sized balls, then use your hands to shape into sausages.

**7** Place the pan over a medium heat. Brush the sausages all over with a little oil. Add to the pan and fry for 5–10 minutes, turning occasionally, until golden brown all over (you might need to do this in batches).

**8** Tip the potatoes back into the pan and mash with a potato masher until you can't see any lumps. Stir in the dairy-free spread, 1–2 splashes of milk and a little salt and pepper. Mash until well mixed and smooth.

**9** Spoon the mashed potato onto plates. Place the sausages on top and serve.

Main meals

# THAI GREEN CURRY

## Ingredients

200g firm tofu, drained
1 tbsp vegetable oil
bunch of spring onions, trimmed and sliced
small bunch of coriander, leaves picked and stalks finely chopped
1 red pepper, deseeded and sliced
75g baby corn, halved lengthways
4 tbsp Thai green curry paste
1 x 400ml can coconut milk
1 lime, zest and juice

75g sugar snap peas
200g long-grain rice

TO SERVE
1 lime, cut into wedges

SERVES 4

Kids Can Cook Vegetarian

**1** Put the tofu between 2 clean tea towels and place a heavy pan on top (this will help to draw out the moisture). Set aside.

**2** Meanwhile, heat the oil in a large pan over a medium heat. Fry the spring onions and coriander stalks for 3 minutes, stirring regularly, until soft.

**3** Add the pepper and corn to the pan and stir-fry for 5 minutes, or until starting to soften.

**4** Stir in the curry paste. Cook for 2 minutes, stirring regularly.

**5** Add the coconut milk, lime zest and juice.

**6** Cut the tofu into 2½cm cubes. Add to the pan, along with the sugar snap peas. Bring to the boil, then turn the heat to low. Bubble gently for 10 minutes, or until the sugar snap peas are soft and the sauce has thickened.

**7** While the curry is cooking, make the rice. Put the rice in a sieve and rinse under the cold tap.

**8** Tip the rice into a pan and cover with cold water. Bring to the boil, then turn down the heat until bubbling gently. Put the lid on. Cook for 10 minutes, or until tender. Remove from the heat, drain off any remaining water and set aside for a few minutes.

**9** Add the coriander leaves to the curry. Serve with the rice and lime wedges.

Main meals **49**

# KATSU CURRY

## Ingredients

vegetable oil, for greasing
100g plain flour, sifted
300ml unsweetened soya milk
50g plain flour
150g panko breadcrumbs, crushed
1 large cauliflower, cut into florets
salt and pepper

FOR THE CURRY SAUCE
1 tbsp vegetable oil
2 tsp mild curry powder
1 tsp ground turmeric
1 onion, finely sliced
2 garlic cloves, crushed

SERVES 4-6

1 x thumb-sized piece of root ginger, peeled and grated
1 x 400ml can coconut milk
2 tbsp soy sauce

TO SERVE
1 x quantity cooked rice (see page 49)
½ carrot
¼ cucumber

**1** Heat the oven to 220°C/fan 200°C/gas mark 7. Grease 2 large baking trays.

**2** Tip 100g flour into a large bowl and make a hole in the middle. Pour a little of the milk into the hole and whisk in a little flour from the sides. Continue, adding the milk a little at a time, until all the milk is used up and you have a smooth batter.

**3** Put 2 wide, shallow bowls on the work surface. Tip 50g flour into one and the breadcrumbs into the other. Season the flour with salt and pepper.

Kids Can Cook Vegetarian

**4** Dip a cauliflower floret into the flour, then into the batter, and then coat in breadcrumbs. Place on a baking tray. Repeat with the rest of the cauliflower. Bake for 30–35 minutes, or until the cauliflower is tender and the coating is golden brown.

**5** While the cauliflower nuggets are cooking, heat the oil in a large frying pan over a medium heat. Add the curry powder and turmeric. Cook for 2 minutes, stirring regularly.

**6** Turn the heat to low. Add the onion, garlic and ginger. Cook for 10–15 minutes, or until soft.

**7** Pour in the coconut milk. Bubble gently for 15 minutes, then stir in the soy sauce. While the sauce is cooking, make the rice (see page 49).

**8** Use a vegetable peeler to make long ribbons of carrot and cucumber.

**9** Place a large spoonful of rice onto each plate. Top with curry sauce, cauliflower nuggets and vegetable ribbons.

Main meals **51**

# MIXED BEAN CHILLI

## Ingredients
2 tbsp olive oil
1 red onion, finely chopped
2 garlic cloves, crushed
½ tbsp ground paprika
½ tbsp ground cumin
2 tsp mild chilli powder
2 x 400g cans chopped tomatoes
pinch of sugar
1 x 400g can kidney beans, drained and rinsed
1 x 400g can black beans, drained and rinsed

TO SERVE
1 x quantity cooked rice (see page 49)
grated vegetarian Cheddar cheese

SERVES 4

**1** Heat the oil in a large pan over a low heat. Fry the onion for 5–10 minutes until soft.

**2** Stir in the garlic, paprika, cumin and chilli powder. Cook for 1 minute.

**3** Add the tomatoes and sugar. Turn up the heat, bring to the boil, then turn the heat to low. Put a lid on the pan and bubble gently for 20 minutes. While the chilli is cooking, make the rice (see page 49).

**4** Stir the beans into the chilli. Cook without a lid for 5 minutes.

**5** Divide the rice between 4 plates or bowls. Spoon over the chill and sprinkle with a little grated cheese.

## Variation
Try serving the chilli with baked potatoes, quinoa, couscous or fresh bread, or inside a burrito or taco.

EXTRA TOPPING IDEAS
* sliced avocado * Guacamole (see page 9)
* tortilla chips * salsa * vegetarian sour cream
* lime wedges

Main meals 53

# BLUEBERRY PANCAKES

## Ingredients
200g self-raising flour
1 tsp baking powder
1 egg
300ml milk
knob of unsalted butter, melted, plus extra for frying
150g blueberries

MAKES 8-10

**1** Sift the flour and baking powder into a large bowl. Using a wooden spoon, make a large hole in the middle of the flour.

**2** Crack the egg into a jug. Add the milk. Beat together with a fork until smooth.

**3** Pour a little egg mixture into the middle of the flour. Bring some flour into the middle. Whisk until smooth. Continue until the egg mixture is used up and you have a smooth batter.

**4** Stir in the melted butter and blueberries.

**5** Heat a little butter in a large pan over a medium heat. Drop in tablespoonfuls of batter, leaving space between each one (you'll need to cook 3 or 4 at a time).

**6** Cook for 2–3 minutes, or until small bubbles appear on the surface of each pancake.

**7** Flip over with a fish slice. Cook for 2 minutes until golden and firm. Serve with maple or golden syrup.

# BANANA PANCAKES

## Ingredients
2 very ripe bananas
2 eggs
120g self-raising flour
vegetable oil, for frying

MAKES 8-10

### Variation
For vegan pancakes, replace the eggs with 2 tbsp dairy-free milk.

**1** In a large bowl, mash the bananas with a fork until smooth.

**2** Whisk in the eggs.

**3** Sift in the flour. Whisk until well mixed.

**4** Heat a little oil in a large pan over a medium heat. Drop in tablespoonfuls of batter, leaving space between each one (you'll need to cook 3 or 4 at a time).

**5** Cook for 2–3 minutes, or until small bubbles appear on the surface of each pancake.

**6** Flip over with a fish slice. Cook for 2 minutes until golden and firm. Serve with maple or golden syrup.

Sweet treats

# COURGETTE BROWNIES

Adding grated courgette to chocolate brownies makes them super fudgy and moist. They'll keep for up to 4 days in an airtight container, or you can freeze them for up to a month.

## Ingredients
125ml vegetable oil, plus extra for greasing
300g caster sugar
250g plain flour
50g cocoa powder
1½ tsp bicarbonate of soda
pinch of salt
250g courgette, grated

MAKES 12

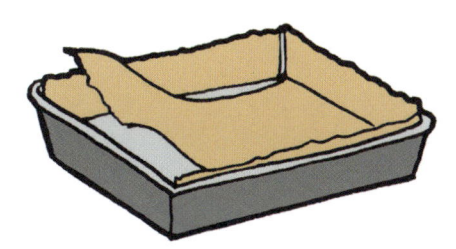

**1** Heat the oven to 180°C/fan 160°C/gas mark 4. Grease a 22 x 33cm baking tray and line it with baking paper.

**2** In a large bowl, whisk together the oil and sugar.

**3** Sift in the flour, cocoa powder, bicarbonate of soda and salt. Fold in with a large metal spoon until well mixed.

**4** Gently fold in the courgette.

**5** Spoon into the tin and smooth the top. Bake for 25–30 minutes until just firm in the centre.

**6** Leave to cool in the tin before cutting into squares.

## Variation

Courgette isn't the only vegetable you can add to brownies. You could try grated carrot or parsnip instead.

Sweet treats

# BUTTERNUT SQUASH COOKIES

## Ingredients
200g dairy-free spread
200g caster sugar
125g soft dark brown sugar
½ butternut squash, roasted and cooled (see Tip, page 23)
325g plain flour, sifted, plus extra for dusting
100g rolled oats
1 tsp baking powder
¾ tsp bicarbonate of soda
1 tsp salt
1 tsp mixed spice (optional)

FOR THE ICING
125g icing sugar, sifted
5 tsp lemon juice

MAKES 24

**1** Beat together the dairy-free spread, caster sugar and brown sugar in a large bowl, using a wooden spoon or electric whisk, until pale and fluffy.

**2** Scoop out the butternut squash flesh and put 150g into a bowl. Mash with a fork until smooth.

**3** Stir the mashed squash into the butter and sugar mixture.

**4** Fold in the flour, oats, baking powder, bicarbonate of soda, salt and mixed spice (if using).

**5** Bring the dough together into a ball. Cover in plastic wrap and put in the refrigerator for 1 hour.

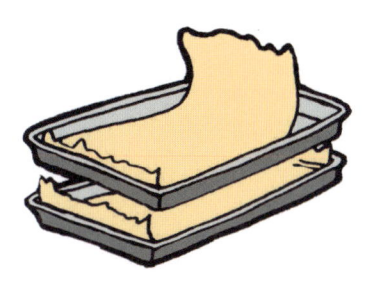

**6** Heat the oven to 200°C/fan 180°C/gas mark 6. Line 2 baking trays with baking paper.

**7** Dust your hands and the work surface with flour. Roll the dough into 24 evenly sized balls (about the size of a golf ball). Place on the baking trays, leaving space between each one.

**8** Bake for 15 minutes. Allow to cool on the trays for a few minutes, then transfer to a wire rack to cool.

**9** Once cool, make the icing. Put the icing sugar in a small bowl. Stir in the lemon juice a little at a time until the icing is smooth and glossy.

**10** Drizzle or pipe the icing on in a zigzag pattern.

Sweet treats

# CHOCOLATE & BEETROOT CAKE

## Ingredients

200ml vegetable oil, plus extra for greasing
215g cooked beetroot (in natural juices, not vinegar), chopped
2 eggs
175g plain flour
75g cocoa powder
2 tsp baking powder
225g caster sugar

FOR THE FROSTING
50g unsalted butter, softened
200g icing sugar, sifted
100g full-fat cream cheese

Kids Can Cook Vegetarian

**1** Heat the oven to 200°C/fan 180°C/gas mark 6. Grease 2 x 20cm sandwich tins and line the bases with baking paper.

**2** Put the oil, beetroot and eggs in a food processor. Blend until smooth. Tip into a large bowl.

**3** Sift in the flour, cocoa powder and baking powder. Tip in the caster sugar. Fold in with a large metal spoon until well mixed. Divide equally between the tins.

**4** Bake for 20–25 minutes, or until a skewer inserted into the centre comes out clean. Allow to cool in the tins, then turn out onto a wire rack.

**5** To make the frosting, put the butter in a bowl. Beat in the icing sugar a little at a time, using a wooden spoon or electric whisk, until smooth.

**6** Beat in half the cream cheese. Add the rest and beat until smooth.

**7** Once the cakes are completely cool, spread some frosting onto one cake with a palette knife. Place the other cake on top. Use the rest of the frosting to cover the top and sides.

### Tip

To decorate the cake, dust with 1-2 tbsp sifted cocoa powder or grate over a little dark chocolate.

Sweet treats

# FRUIT & ROOT ROLL-UPS

Fruit roll-ups (sometimes called fruit leathers) are easy to prepare, but they do need a long time in the oven. It can take up to 5 hours for them to dry out, so why not get creative with some fruit and vegetables while you wait? (See Tip.)

## Ingredients
600g frozen strawberries
200g carrot, chopped
2 Braeburn or Gala apples, cored and cut into chunks

MAKES 10-12

**1** Line 2 baking trays with baking paper.

**2** Put the strawberries, carrot and apple in a large pan. Place over a low heat and cover with a lid. Cook for 30 minutes, or until the carrot and apple are soft.

Kids Can Cook Vegetarian

**3** Remove from the heat and allow to cool a little. Tip into a food processor. Blend to a smooth purée.

**4** Using a wooden spoon, push the purée through a sieve into a clean pan.

**5** Put the pan over a medium heat. Cook, stirring occasionally, for about 10 minutes, or until thickened. When it's ready, you should be able to pull the spoon through the purée and see the bottom of the pan.

**6** Heat the oven to its lowest setting. Divide the mixture between the trays, spreading the purée out thinly and evenly. Bake for 3–5 hours, or until it's no longer sticky, but is still bendy.

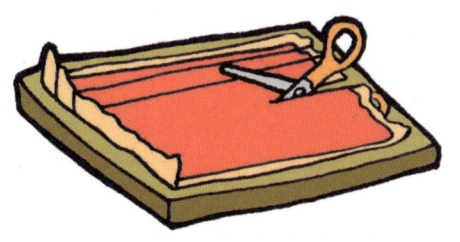

**7** Cut into strips using a pizza cutter or scissors (make sure you cut through the paper too).

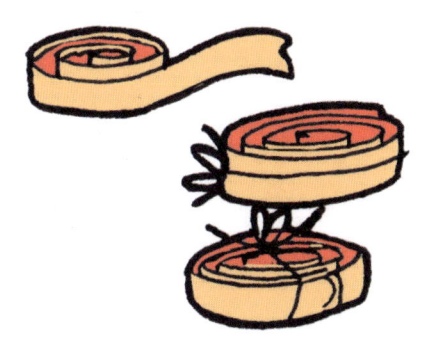

**8** Roll up and tie with string. Store in an airtight container.

## Tip

While you wait, have a go at creating some colourful prints with fruit and vegetables. You could use trimmings for this, such as the base of a pepper or a broccoli stem, or fruits that are past their best. Just cut them up to create interesting shapes, dip them in paint and print onto paper. The bottom half of a baby gem lettuce makes a lovely rose, and you can use orange halves to create a striking tie-dye effect.

Sweet treats

First published 2022 by Button Books, an imprint of Guild of Master Craftsman Publications Ltd. Text © GMC Publications Ltd, 2022. Copyright in the Work © GMC Publications Ltd, 2022. Illustrations © Esther Coombs, 2022. Recipes by Laura Paton. ISBN 978 1 78708 118 5. All rights reserved. The right of Esther Coombs © to be identified as the illustrator of this work has been asserted in accordance with the Copyright, Designs and Patents Act 1988, sections 77 and 78. No part of this publication may be reproduced, stored in a retrieval system, or transmitted in any form or by any means without the prior permission of the publisher and copyright owner. This book is sold subject to the condition that all designs are copyright and are not for commercial reproduction without the permission of the designer and copyright owner. The publishers and author can accept no legal responsibility for any consequences arising from the application of information, advice or instructions given in this publication. A catalogue record for this book is available from the British Library. Printed and bound in China.

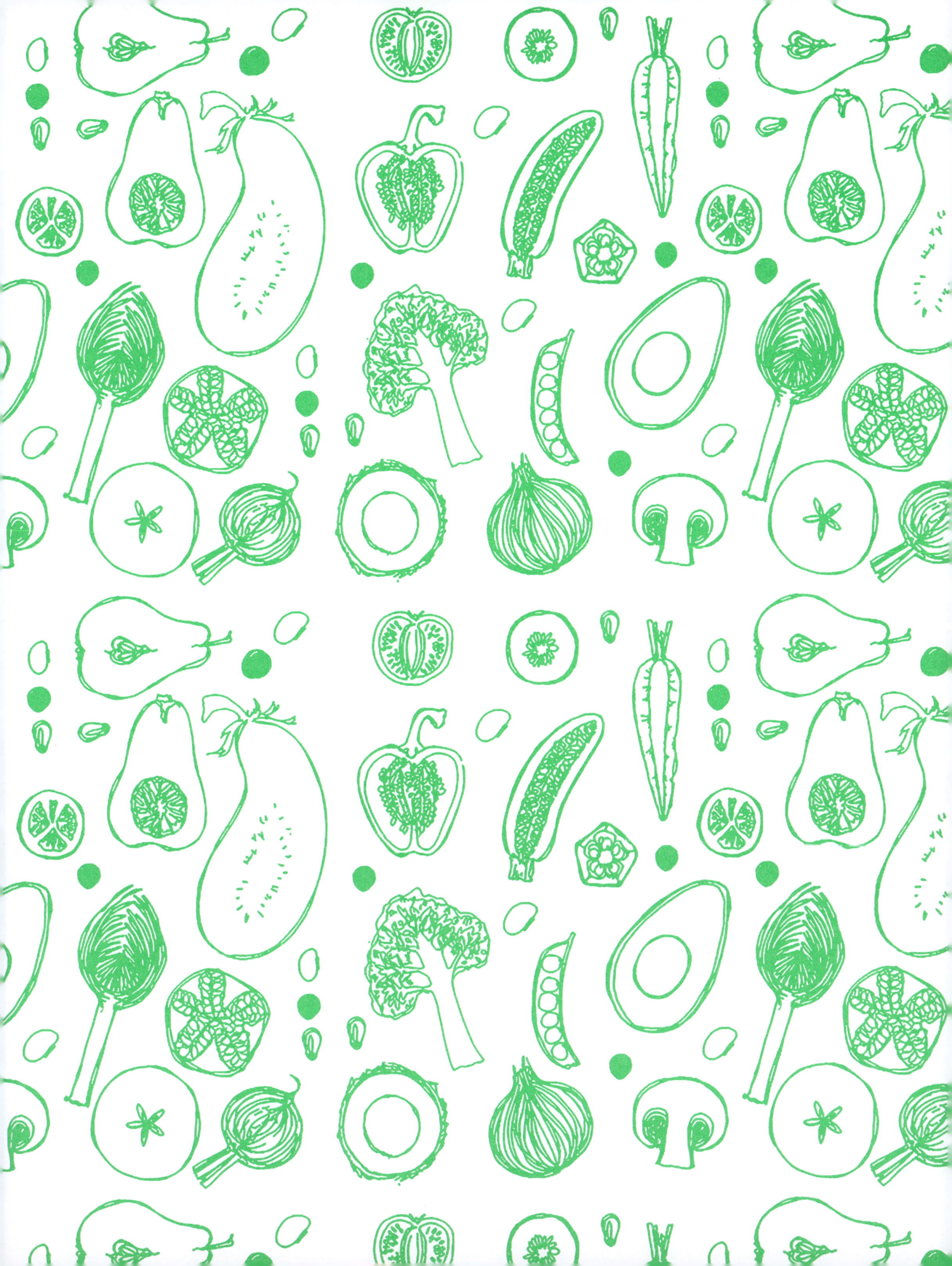

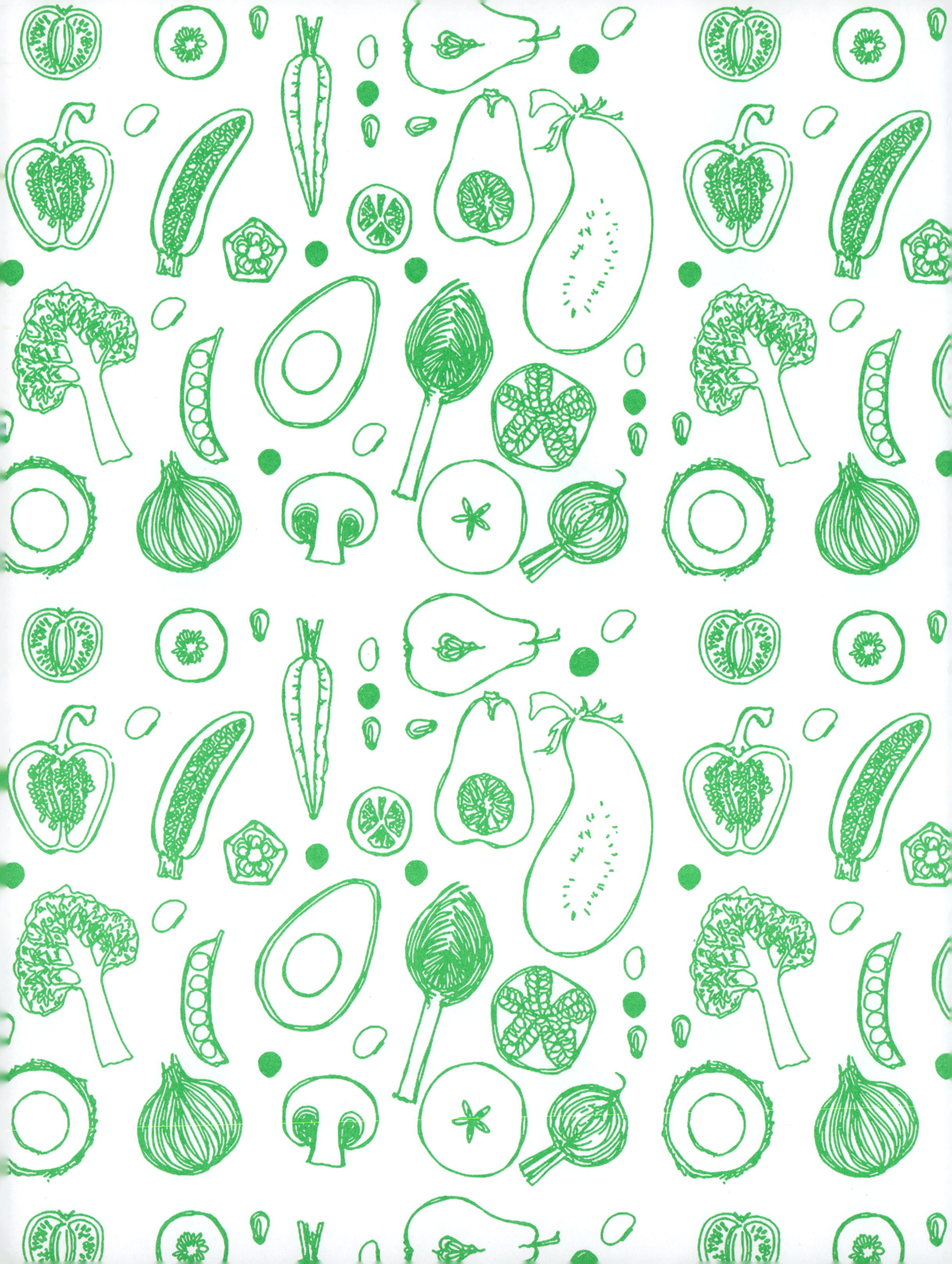